SPRINGTIME

Impressions of a Young Mind

SPRINGTIME

Impressions of a
Young Mind

Poetess
Aanchal Gupta

Penman Books

Office No. 303, Kumar House Building,
D Block, Central Market, Opp PVR Cinema,
Prashant Vihar, Delhi 110085, India

Website: www.penmanbooks.com
Email: publish@penmanbooks.com

First Published by Penman Books 2020
Copyright © Aanchal Gupta 2020
All Rights Reserved.

Title: Springtime: Impressions of a Young Mind
ISBN: 978-93-90156-05-4

Acknowledgements

I am deeply grateful to my parents and my brother for their loving support, encouragement, and guidance without which this book could never have been created in the first place. My father acted as the lighthouse that guided my novice ship through the waters of self-publishing; my mother gave me the emotional support and confidence to put my thoughts into words, and my ever-supportive brother helped with formulating & editing my expressions. My family has always brainstormed ideas and thoughts with me that get my thought engine running at full speed, allowing me to express my thoughts with clarity by questioning various aspects of my endeavours.

I would like to thank my aunts Ms Upasana Singh, Mrs Tripti Gupta and Mrs Sandesh Jindal, for the motivating feedback that they have given me with regard to my poems.

I am thankful to all the family friends who have supported my writing ventures; my father's friends: Brigadier (Retd.) Y.V.R. Vijay, Colonel Vikram Bhushan, Colonel Vikas

Puri and Mr Ashok Jha; my mother's friends: Mrs Lavanya Vijay, Mrs Rajni Rao, Mrs Sneha Jha, Mrs Avantika, Mrs Vaishali Seth, Mrs Akanksha Agnihotri, Mrs Meenakshi Ahuja and Mrs Rashmi Jha.

I have had the fortune to be taught by dedicated and exceptional teachers who enabled me to translate my emotions into expressions. My revered school Principal, the late Mala Jetly Ma'am, was the heart and soul of my school who always had a kind word to say in every situation, with a benevolent smile upon her fair face. She encouraged all of us to grow and reach for ever-increasing heights with even the sky not being the limit.

I would like to attribute my literary skills to my English teachers, Richika Grover Ma'am and Sukhjeet Kaur Ma'am, who have helped me to expand and refine my capabilities, be it in literature, grammar or creative writing. Their drive to make me realise my full potential and periodic appreciation have enabled me to attain my confidence level. They have enabled me to connect beyond the boundaries of the textbook by bringing to light the various facets of life and emotions through avid discussions and lively stories.

My collection of seventy-five plus poems wouldn't have been possible if my Political Science teacher, Kavya Anklekar Ma'am, hadn't asked me that one day (26th

August 2016) in the school library to write a few lines about my brother for his 10ᵗʰ-grade farewell oration. This impromptu request resulted in my first poem (*My Brother Rahul*), heralding the coming of many more poems.

My fluency and expressions in Hindi can be credited to my Hindi teacher, Manju Pant Ma'am, to whom I'm deeply grateful for being a motherly figure as well as my class teacher of 2 years.

Friends are one of the biggest supporters of a person, and mine are not an exception. I'm grateful to have the support of Kavana Anklekar, Hiya Pandey, Keertana Sharma, Khushi Agrawal, Akriti Vatal, Priya Dharavat, Vrushti Shah, Rashmi Pai, Muskan Bagdiya, Arpita Rai, Khushi Puri and Vaishnavi Didi who have motivated me through their encouraging words and helpful suggestions.

I would like to thank my publisher Mr Tarun Singh, Mr Neeraj Sharma and the Penman Books Team for helping me in my journey to successfully publish this book.

Foreword

I can vividly recall the Friday evening, sometime in August 2006, when I came back from the office and hugged my three year old daughter Aanchal. After I freshened myself, and was having evening tea with family, she shared her experience of my beard pinching her soft cheeks in the form of a four lines poem:

डैडी की दाढ़ी आई

बच्चों को चुभी

बच्चों ने कहा

उई! उई! उई!

My wife Arti and I, were pleasantly surprised to discover her innate talent – the ability to express her thoughts and feelings with rhyming words.

As years passed by, we had several occasions, where we found her expressions flowing out in a similar manner – rhyming sentences instead of plain words/sentences. We realised the hidden seed inside her, just waiting for the right soil and sunshine to sprout. This talent was also noticed by her teachers and friends in the school. One day, her teacher asked Aanchal to write a poem on her brother, Rahul for his school farewell function. This was in the year 2016. Her poem received great accolades from his friends and teachers. This was a turning point for her inner confidence and self-belief. We all knew that the seed had sprouted and with time will grow bigger and stronger. Her first poem '*My Brother Rahul*' has been included in this book.

As Father of Aanchal Gupta, it gives me a great sense of pleasure and pride to write the Foreword for my daughter's first compilation of poems in the book '*SPRINGTIME – Impressions of a Young Mind*'. Undoubtedly, it's a great feat for a seventeen year old girl to express the kaleidoscope/ bouquet of emotions, she has gone through her life in these poems. What I liked most in her poems, is the spontaneity of thoughts and expressions. There have been many times, especially in the late evenings while talking with her mother, she will suddenly get a spark of an idea, a train of thoughts and a yearning desire to pen down her thoughts. This aspect has been brought out by her, by including the context she has written after each poem, so that the meaning and subtlety of each word and expression can be savoured.

In her unique way, Aanchal has arranged this bouquet of emotions into various sections related to a particular feeling such as Romance, Family, Nature, etc., and has also associated it with a flower, which represents the same. She has been a keen, observant and voracious reader and has a good vocabulary (often called '*Dictionary*' in her class by her classmates). This can be seen in her poems, whereby she has captured various hues and colours of daily life moments in rhyming words.

I am sure that each poem will rekindle some memory or thought or experience in your life, as well. An easy to read collection for all ages, this book will certainly create value in your book collection. It can be read during any of your emotional states, and I am sanguine that it will bring a smile to your face.

Vinay Gupta

Proud Father of Aanchal Gupta, the Poetess

Dedication

"To my family of four..."

Introduction

Having been born and raised in an Army family, my loving parents and older brother are my best friends to whom I can talk to about everything. We, as a family, are a gregarious lot who love to meet and connect with people, play cards and badminton in the evenings, go for family walks and last, but not the least, have spontaneous and interactive discussions on anything and everything around us. Others may have marathon movie sessions but me? My mother and I can have marathon talk sessions that can last anywhere between 20 minutes to 2 hours because we absolutely love to talk.

So, it probably doesn't come across as a surprise that most of my poems can be traced back to the happenings around this family unit of mine. While discussing a particular topic, watching a movie, attending a function, having a stomach-ache or just plain thinking, a sudden thought comes to my mind that gets my creative juices flowing and results in me frantically trying to somehow record it somewhere before it slips away from my consciousness.

It may be on a piece of paper or on one of my family WhatsApp chats (which I use as a notepad) or on my phone's voice recorder if the inspiration strikes me at midnight and I'm too sleepy to actually type or jot it down (which it has if you read this book).

While writing or typing a new poem, I often ask my family which line would fit in better or would be more meaningful when I'm faced with two lines, and I cannot decide which one to add (I'm a Gemini, so being in a dilemma comes naturally, I guess).

I love using literary devices such as Alliteration, Metaphor, Repetition and Personification, so you will come across them often; the titles of many of my poems are examples of alliteration. I also like to experiment and change up things, in the poems I write as well as in experimenting with the local dishes of the places we visit or reside in, making new mocktails and desserts with my family.

I'm notorious among my classmates for long-winded explanations, but I guess you can already see that ;)

My poems explore a variety of subjects ranging from wishes, marriage, romance, humour and hope, to sensitive issues of our society, lifestyle and sadness.

I hope that you will enjoy reading them as much as I've enjoyed writing them.

Aanchal Gupta
The Author

A Note to the Reader

*Flowers have a unique way of expressing even
the unspoken feelings that we hold deep in our hearts.
Poetry gives voice to these feelings too.*

I thought, why not combine and connect the two somehow? Leehama's webtoon *Gourmet Hound* with its food-themed character names inspired me to have flower-themed section names.

Contents

Section I
Hydrangea (Emotions)

Hydrangeas symbolize various emotions depending upon their colours such as heartfelt gratitude (pink), desire to deeply understand someone (purple), boastfulness/vanity (white), and frigidity/apology (blue).

An Unfulfilled Hope

Humpty Dumpty rolled down a slope,
Broke all his bones, lost all his hope.
All this misery for he was a dope!

Is there a chance for him? Nope!
No! He won't be able to cope.

Was pushed down the slope,
For with the countess he had tried to elope.

The Count crushed all their hope,
Bound Humpty with a rope,
And rolled him down the slope!

Caught during their lope,
Quite near that very slope.

After this fiasco 'n' opera soap
The Contessa was kept under a microscope,
Where all she did was mope.
Still, in her heart, she nurtured a little hope.

Meanwhile, Humpty was forced to walk a tightrope,
With bruises similar to a kaleidoscope.
He also got quite familiar with the stethoscope.

On a later date, came an envelope,
Declaring Humpty's demise due to a microbe.
About this, the countess had read in her horoscope,
This misery, a fatal blow with which she had to cope,
When all she had was an Unfulfilled Hope.

28th February 2018; 22:22

I had a random thought about the nursery rhyme while watching the movie The Mask of Zorro (when Captain Harrison Love tumbles down a slope in the climax). An impulsive action on my part to imagine an affair between Humpty and a countess as a joke resulted in this. I tried for comic drama (my first try), but it is up to you.

A Long-Awaited Day

For this day, I have waited long,
To start something creative, my desire's strong.
Tomorrow I tumble into mischief headlong.
This day awaited has finally come along!

21st December 2017, 22:14

My exams had just ended that day, and my winter holidays were to begin from the next day; so, my excitement came out in the form of this short poem. Thanks.

Laughter: A Panacea for Stress!

Laughter is a stress buster,
Which helps you regain your lustre.

It increases blood circulation,
Helps you release many a frustration

It cleanses lungs and body tissues,
And lets you calmly deal with your issues.

So, with all the strength that you can muster,
Laugh, for the answer is Laughter!

23rd March 2018, 18:32.

I wrote this to supplement an email of mine, to lighten up a friend's spirits during exams.

Lucky Thirteen

No loss, no gain.
No profit, no pain;
When all collect their due,
And protests are few.

If at this game you're new,
Well, my friend, let me explain it to you!

To 4 players in playing keen,
Cards dealt (to each) are thirteen.
Not popularity, but of mind's kind of scene,
Is what this game is that I've seen.

The rules are easy to glean,
4 bundles of rewards shine a sheen.

No use in being mean,
Keep calm, stay serene.

There're many combos made in between,
Ace, king & queen,
And 4, 3, 2 that let you preen,
When you match the highest trio, a win clean.

We call it the Lucky Thirteen,
Where with brains you make sense out of chaos:
A trail, a Sequence, a Colour ranging between
Spade to Club, Black or Red; not Green,
A Pair or the Highest card you quarantine.

It makes you wonder about possibilities unforeseen,
And cry out 'Oh, Luck! Where have you been?!'

The winner takes a bundle for each round won.
Thus ensues a game of fun,
Where Luck 'n' Life, Talent 'n' Time, take a turn.

So, are you game?
This could be your rise to fame,
'Cause you'll never be the same.

6th October 2018, 22:48.

I finally wrote a poem after so many days of wondering
when the next one will get the jump on me. I was playing
cards with my family, a routine occurrence on Saturday

nights. We were playing what we call Lucky Thirteen 'n' each one of us won back the bundle of 4 cards (representing money) that we had put forward as a reward. That is what inspired me to write this poem. I have always loved playing cards and want others (who don't know about them) to play too. It is a fun way to unwind.

I, Me and Myself

There's more to me than meets the eye,
Get to know me to answer why.

In academics, I'm studious.
With promises, I'm fastidious.
With a reputation sincere,
Of which everyone's made me aware.
I possess many a layer,
And want everyone to be fair.

I love literature,
Books and poems, in my mind, are a fixture.

I've an Army background,
Due to which, with manners am I bound.

I love to sing,
And many times, to a single song I cling
Not many understand my humour,

For them, my jokes are lame,
They spread many a nasty rumour,
But for my family, I live up to my name.

My passion is reading,
My thoughts on paper bleeding.

With an appearance misleading,
Many a person do I confuse,
My nature has left many reeling,
Due to the preconceived notions they choose.

For, there's more to me than meets the eye,
Get to know me to answer why.

11th December 2017, 12:14

It was an activity given in school: write an autobiographical poem in 10 minutes. The result is in front of you.

I, Me and Myself Darker

I've a few qualities I deeply despise,
That often irritate me like lice.
I always try to be nice,
But I know that may not suffice,
For, these qualities are attention-seeking, I surmise.
But don't write me off,
Cause everybody's got faults,
These are mine, the golden time halts.
For this, many may at me scoff,
But please don't write me off.
Responsibility I unintentionally shirk,
When temptation does in the shadows lurk.
Alas, this harmful tendency is hereditary,
I try to but this I can't bury.
I can't help but feel guilt,
For wishing this wasn't the way I'm built.

1st January 2018, 19:34

As you can probably guess, this is the dark version of my previous autobiographical poem, 'I, Me and Myself'. I wrote this when I was feeling extremely bad about myself and had had a serious dressing down from my parents. I have a bad habit of binge-reading novels and have finished a new novel in one day often. They are the temptation that I am referring to in the above poem.

These Years Have Flown By

These years have flown by,
One minute a hi
The other a goodbye.
With moments both good and wry.

These years have flown by,
As I walk down memory lane whereby,
I can see in my mind's eye,
That friend who could, with a humour sly,
Break the ice with a newcomer shy.

These years have flown by,
Finding ourselves is what we try,
Unlocking secrets, figuring out where our futures lie.

These years have flown by,
I tell you this with a sigh,
Don't spend every moment asking why
Live every moment to the fullest, dear friend my,

For you never know when the time will fly,
And you will be left wondering how these years
have flown by.

19th February 2018, 23:06 pm.

I wrote this poem when a thought had struck me suddenly: I am in 9th grade going to be in 10th grade next month onwards! Where have the years flown by?! And that was the beginning of this impromptu poem. I have tried something new (for me that is), starting every stanza with the title line. I was a bit apprehensive at first but found the result quite good. I hope you do too.

The Beauty of a Book

Stacked together on a wooden shelf,
Each book tells its own tale.
With a binding and cover to show itself,
And an aroma you never want to exhale.

Pick one up to discover its secrets,
A treasure of knowledge be it yours or mine.
A whole new world in which one forgets,
Rationality and reason; a world divine.

Bookshelves may take up just a few floors,
But the wisdom that they so freely bestow,
Can open up so many doors,
And can make even loneliness go.

So, during this lockdown,
Pick up a book,
Put up your feet,
And get ready for an immersive read!

12th April 2020, 16:53

Picture prompt 6

I wrote this poem as part of an online workshop conducted by The Stolen Script of which my friend is a part. We were given 6 pictorial prompts and had to write a poem on any one of those in 30 minutes. The prompt that spoke to me was the last one: 2 rows of bookshelves in a golden yet dimly lit room. What can I say? I love reading! I hope you enjoy it.

Repent to Reinvent

These last few days,
I had been feeling pretty low;
Tried to cheer myself up in many ways,
But never quite felt inspiration flow,
Flow to draw, dance or write.
I felt out of it,
A fish out of water ain't right,
Wondering what has made me lose it?

The traits that defined me once,
So proud and proficient they always made me feel,
Have faded away, leaving me a dunce,
With nothing left to do but reel,
From this reality, I had never expected to see,
For having taken my own self, personality, for granted,
For not knowing how lucky I have been,
To be born naturally talented.
Not until the last talent had bid goodbye,
Not until I felt rung dry;
By losing to temptation,

I lost the satisfaction studies brought.
Learnt the hard way to be wary of wayward paths,
Give in once, and the descent deep down starts.

At last, I see the light,
A beacon of hope that there's still time,
To make wrongs right,
To turn things back as they were, sublime!

Off the tempting path, I go,
Cause the time for temptation is past;
If I don't today eradicate this slithering shadow,
I can't make my fading bright future last,
And may slip further into its greying grasp.

This, right now, is my moment,
A moment to get back who I had been;
A moment to repent and reinvent;
To become a better version than I've ever seen;
So that I'm proud to say my time was well-spent.

4th and 5th April 2020

(From 21:16 of 4th April till 00:15 of 5th April)

I wrote this poem when at home due to the Covid-19 lockdown. Since the last 3 months, it felt like all my enthusiasm for studies (which have been a big source of enjoyment for me since early childhood, I mean I loved going to school), art, music, etc., had drained away, leaving me unmotivated and out of sorts. Formerly exciting schoolwork seemed like an ever-increasing burden with the advent of 12th grade since March 3 and then quarantine closed my school just 10 days after that. I've been a topper who submitted assignments early or on time but now I feel like I've become a slacker who procrastinates a lot and hands in work late, a reality I'm frankly not used to and one I don't like. I thought that these traits which established me as a 'scholar' would remain with me ever long, but an addiction to WEBTOONS has taken me off the right and responsible track in just 8 months so I was gravely wrong. But now I plan to consciously cultivate these precious lost traits of mine again that once came to me effortlessly. I felt lighter today, so I wrote this, and I hope it might help someone in a similar situation like me to not give up on themselves. Thanks.

Questions

Questions bring clarity,
Questions dispel vanity;

Questions bring forth the truth,
Questions are the nature of the youth;

Questions indicate our living existence,
Questions show passion and persistence;

Questions can leave a mark,
Questions lighten the ignorant dark;

Questions can unlock minds,
Questions are asked by masterminds;

Questions form a person's sanity,
Questions can save humanity.

20th March 2020, 20:27.

*I guess you might be QUESTIONING (sorry for being punny)
why I wrote this poem or what led to it: I had realised that*

questions do indeed bring clarity a long time back and had the first line in my head since then, a line which I decided to put down to paper. I try to experiment with my poems quite often, so this time I have tried to write a poem with each line starting with the same word, i.e. 'Questions'. Well, I hope you like it. Thanks.

7 Days of Holiday Heaven

If only my throat wasn't sore,
I guess I could enjoy some more,
These seven days of holiday,
That will to 12th grade give way.
But I can spend them in many a way,
For who's to say, how I should spend them anyway?
I could sing, I could draw, I could dance,
To fully avail myself of this rare chance!

Reading books of action, drama and romance;
Revisiting eagerly awaited but never seen movies;
Binge-watching a brand-new series;
It seems that my wish list keeps growing,
As fast as the river of time is flowing.

Holidays, a period of games and gaiety,
We all know, they never fail to entrance.
I hope to maintain this stress-free stance,
Throughout the coming academic year,
With energy, and a focus crystal clear.

27th February 2020, 13:00

I wrote this poem after my final exams of 11th grade ended. I now have 7 days of holidays before the new academic session starts on 5th March 2020. I'm going to thoroughly enjoy them with my family because these exams had been especially stressful this time: health problems, familial arguments, etc. Thanks.

Heinous Hair Fall

Bane of my existence is my falling hair,
Wherever I look, I see it everywhere;

Forming ever long patterns on the white tiled floor,
Stretching from the bed to the door.

My hip-length hair may be my pride,
Yet it really pains me inside,

To see it copiously falling down.
I hope every day to not become a bald clown,

Wishing to have a full head of hair,
Cause heinous hair fall sure ain't fair.

Each strand may be straight, soft and fine,
I'm thankful, but I wish it would thicken,

Into a bountiful mass like before.
This is just a wish of mine,
To not be hair fall stricken even more.

22nd February 2020, 10:25

As you can guess, I wrote this poem out of frustration and sadness that almost every day, I lose around 1/6th of my already thin hair, despite combing it carefully. I think I'll have to cut it soon...till my shoulders maybe? Thanks.

Memories

Though we may make memories,
It is memories that make up us.

Helping us sort through the histories,
That we share with each other,
To respond accordingly to one another,
They dispel the past's mysteries.

The backbone of thoughts and opinions,
Of which, we are mere minions,
These memories are quite a powerful entity,
That determines whether your life be (deemed)
complete or empty.

13th February 2020, 11:28

Extended from 1st 2 lines on 5th April 2020, 23:14

Inspired by Moon Valley, a WEBTOON where the protagonist's very personality changes due to amnesia and lost memories that were never completely recovered....a loss that erased an essential friendship with a close one; our memories direct our behaviour and the loss of hers greatly impacted her relationships with everyone around her for she didn't remember what kind of memories she had made with each person prior to her accident and hence didn't know how to act. Thanks.

Vicious Vocals

Finally, back from this strenuous field trip,
God, how I wish their vocal cords would rip!
How could they quench their thirst with nary a sip?!
My cries for peace were merely a blip,
On their radar; my teeth in pain, splitting open my lip.
Their throats, I wanted to into submission whip,
As the unending uproar tightened on my ears my grip.

14th December 2019, 20:02

Writing poems usually helps me express and release my emotions and thoughts....hence I wrote this expression of my disjointed thoughts to relieve myself of the anger, helplessness and headache that had been plaguing me after having to listen (endure) 7 hours of people singing during the whole bus ride (3.5 hrs each side). It was especially horrible after a jam-packed tiring experience at the field trip location, I was reduced to tears during the last 2 hours.

A Truth Bared

Motives matter more than the actions they inspire,
People reveal their true faces in situations dire.
Beware, or you'll be caught in this fierce fire,
Burning bright with lies and lessons of deceit.
These imposters you need to defeat,
If you are to safely land on your feet.

Some people long for lives as lived in novels,
To live happily ever after, they aspire;
They can pretend and act to achieve this desire.
They try to fit in with the notions books portray,
Saying not what they feel, but what they're supposed to say,
In certain situations, to be seen as a certain someone;
Making situations play out in the way they want them to.
Yet, they feel as if it's themselves, they are trying to betray.
Wish I could gift them with pearls of wisdom a few,
But what can I tell myself,
When this feeling is nothing new.

24th January 2020, 18:02

This came out on its own...completely unexpected, like a truth you don't want the people around you to know about you. I feel like I've unburdened myself of this weight of feeling like I'm acting fake, that I've been carrying around since the last 2 years or so. This poem of mine has 2 perspectives: the manipulated and the manipulator. Thanks

Troubling Times

Tensions are running high,
Conflict's constricting the throat of dear family my,
Trouble's brewing, I won't lie.

Finances, feelings are both hurting,
Mistakes 'n' potholes we're unearthing.

How I wish we brave this storm,
Emerging safe and sound,
With that free laughter all around,
Ringing in the house once again,
And tensions going swiftly down the drain.

Surely these are troubling times,
Must make lemonade out of these limes.

21st January 2020, 21:51.

I wrote this poem as tensions are running high in my family right now and I needed an outlet to express this feeling of being fenced in by all sides: final exams in 2 weeks, tests for the whole week, preparing a new song for the farewell in 5 hours, submissions that are due sooner than I could possibly complete my notebooks, etc.

The Sun's Shame

Ba ba burnt skin,
Have you any shame?
Yes sir, yes sir,
It's the sun to blame.

13th July 2018, 14:14.

My retake on a classic nursery rhyme (Ba Ba Black Sheep). Written with respect to the sunburnt skin on my arms. Thanks.

A Noble Soul

She had stars in her eyes,
And thoughts so vast,
Even the universe could not suffice.
She had a conviction steadfast,
Unable to weaken which people she did flabbergast.

Her mouth never uttered lies,
Complete honesty she would exercise.
Her mere presence was nirvana, a paradise,
To be in which one would sacrifice,
Any treasure or any vice!
Such a noble soul never found twice,
To know whom, you will surrender all in a trice.

8th February 2018, 19:27

Inspired by a quote written by my childhood friend Khushi Puri.

An Insect's Warning

It may smell delicious,
May be too good to be true,
Its nature or intentions vicious,
Don't let it get a hold of you
If your nature is capricious,
Don't go near, you may never start new...

10 June 2017, 08:19

I wrote this poem with respect to a Venus flytrap and an insect. You may not believe it, but it was inspired by a plastic container of Yogurt; I was having breakfast at the dining table when I saw the yogurt container in front of me and the word 'delicious' printed on it in bold italics.

Hope That Stays

Be careful with what you wish and say,
For it may be heaven or doomsday,
Depending on where your desires lay.

It's up to you what is and isn't okay,
As it is you who will have to pay,
The price, heavy though it may weigh.

Be careful in what you wish to convey,
Don't let greed lead you astray,
Or you will find to your dismay,
That life isn't a child's play.

It ain't all smiles 'n' laughter gay,
Your high spirits though it may flay,
To know that it contains many a grey.

So, for your good, I pray today,
That your honesty will forever stay,
In darkness, of Hope a penetrating ray!

23rd January 2018, Tuesday, 21:54.

The first 2 lines of this poem came to me while returning home from an evening out. My family and I had been discussing the repercussions of carelessly wishing for selfish desires to come true, a line of thought which prompted me to write this down. Thanks.

An Enigma

There's more to her than meets the eye,
The answer is just out of reach.
So far yet so nigh,
Her barriers so high,
Them you can never breach.

Her past is washed with bleach,
Her present to you only she can teach.
No matter how much you pry,
You in knots will her past tie.
After all, she's scared of a bad guy,
Running away from the sinister spy.
Trying to lay low or she will die!

Your attempts to know will she defy,
Wary of strangers, your curiosity she doesn't buy.
You don't understand why,
Sometimes she does cry.
Others, with a humour dry,
She cracks jokes tainted wry.

The spy, with lies she will ply,
This wild goose chase,
Eats her up and leaves her dry.

With many an alibi,
The police she did mollify.

Your interest she does occupy,
Her aloof nature will mystify,
Many a man to wonder about this stigma,
That wafts off her nature.
This beautiful yet haunted creature,
An enigma.

3rd December 2017

This poem is one of the completely unexpected creations of mine. It came out of nowhere! I guess that it's the result of reading one too many mystery and thriller novels and stories.

An Innocent Accused

An innocent's sanity was tried,
Herself into oblivion, she cried.
No sooner had her tears dried,
She was accused of many people who died.

She's just an innocent accused,
To listen to whose appeal, people refused.
By terrorists, she's being used.
So, help her against being abused.

Lifting the child from the ground,
Faced with snipers, by fear in place she was bound.

Hands above head in the air, she was gagged,
In the back of her mind, worry for her family nagged.

An innocent wrongly caught,
Leaving her family distraught.

"I'm innocent!" she cried,
To her situation, understanding was denied.
Face to face with people who stared,
About her, none of whom cared.
'Make a move, and I'll kill you', the leader dared.
Shaking with fear, she cowered,
In front of the leader, for above her, he towered.

During her walk of unearned shame,
To smithereens, it broke her name,
She has garnered unwanted fame,
Support her, she's an innocent dame.

To court, during the long walk,
Listening to the taunting people talk,
"What did I ever do wrong?" she thinks,
"To have my life destroyed in just a few blinks?
To be accused of terrorist links?"

Someone understood her plight,
Helped her put up a fight.
Saved by the eyewitness who saw,
The innocent saving a child from the terrorist's maw.

Today's the end of D day,
When she was given leeway.

No longer an innocent accused,
"Truth will always win", she mused.

9th July 2017, 14:29

I still cannot believe that I wrote a poem on such a topic! But this is my best poem up till now. That morning, I had just woken up and was looking in the mirror when the 1st stanza of this poem began to create itself in my mind and compelled me to write it down.

Stomach-ache and Slumber

Oh, curse this dreadful stomach-ache,
That's keeping me painfully awake!
Is this the punishment one gets?
Temporary enjoyment and then regrets?
All I did was eat caramel popcorn,
To my heart's content, do I deserve such scorn?
All I wish for is to sleep till morn;
Wake to watch as the sun will adorn,
The lightening sky with its cheer,
And the start of another day becoming clear.
Is comfortable sleep too much to ask for?
Yet no matter how much I crip, complain and cry,
This stomach-ache just isn't willing to say goodbye.

1st May 2020, 23:47

Well, what can I say? I had a dreadful stomach-ache at 23:30 and eyes full of sleep. I just wanted to go to sleep but couldn't due to this pain, hence my frustration came out in the form of this poem. Thanks.

Popping Pimples

Summers bring with them smiles and dipping dimples,
Herald the beginning of fun and vacations;
But they also bring along acne and pimples,
That balance out the euphoric relaxations.

Seems like even pimples wanted to join the party,
With friends like humidity and heat;
They pop up on faces with an enthusiasm hearty,
And a pain that throbs with a pulsing beat.

Need a hand with adding a touch of colour?
Proud pimples are here to save the day!
With a shape that draws your attention,
And a raging red that seems stellar,
They stand out in every possible way!

This summer, let's live and let live,
Enjoy these pimples while they last,
For you can laugh about the stories they give,
When they are lost in the past.

1st May 2020, 21:41

I wrote this poem as my way of laughing at pimples that especially pop up in summers with the onset of heat, humidity and sweat. I was going to take a bath when I brushed aside a strand of hair from my right cheek and felt its pain: I had a new pimple popping its little head out to say hi to summer vacations along with me! The first 2 lines POPPED into my head immediately after this realisation. I hope you enjoy it!

Section II
Rose (Romance)

Rose symbolises various emotions based on its colour: love/romance (red), grace/ admiration (pink), enthusiasm/passion (orange), friendship (yellow) and purity (white)

Pair Perfect

He's the dashing debonair,
She matches him, eye to eye, in flair.
About each other, they deeply care,
Their love possessing many a layer.

Tear them apart, many dare,
But the fools, together do they scare!
Their devotion causing people to wildly stare,
And often many, to at them glare…

'Cause love like their's is found so rare,
That people can't help but want their share.
A dream come true, every woman's prayer,
To have a love so true and fair.

02nd December 2017

My creative juices make sporadic appearances all the time, surprising me every time they do. Today was one such occurrence. I don't know what triggered me into writing this romantic poem and choosing this subject, but I guess it has something to do with my hankering to write a poem/ song for my parent's upcoming 19th Anniversary. Hence, I dedicate this poem to my loving and adoring parents!

A Relationship

What is a relationship?
An arrangement based on companionship,
Can evolve from a friendship,
It's a feeling of kinship.
Each other will one worship,
While in a relationship.

Two have come so far,
One's leaving will leave a scar.
It's difficult we know,
Both phases come, high and low,
No matter what, just don't let go

To quote a line from 'Cold Water',
Saying, "I won't let go",
I know that being your daughter,
That "You won't let go".

14th August 2017

This poem conveys my views on the meaning of a relationship. Obviously, some may say what do I know about them, but I have some idea and have witnessed various kinds of relationships through the interactions between my friends, family, relatives and elders, on which I have based my poem on.

Marriage and Trust

A marriage is based on faith and trust,
Maintaining these is an absolute must.

Both have to earn the other's respect,
Based on their personality and intellect.
Code of conduct, values play an essential role,
In loving the partner of your soul.

Many misunderstandings may arise,
To solve them, your fair faith should suffice.
Allow each to say their piece,
To take decisions with enlightening ease.

May the smiles on your faces be real,
When the camera clicks after a "Cheese!"
And the entwined experiences surreal,
So that it's joy into the world that you release.

20th January 2020, 23:40.

I just came back from attending the wedding of my father's army batchmate's daughter. I guess it's the mood created by that which led me to write this. Thanks.

Section III
Sweet Pea (Greetings)

Sweet pea symbolises pleasure,
gratitude as well as a goodbye
after a pleasant visit.

Happy Birthday, Rockstar Rashmi!

Dear Rashmi,
Not wishing you seemed wrong,
And so I wrote this, couldn't write a song.

You love to dance,
Never missing a chance.

Lively and laughing at things old 'n' new,
Is how I always think of you.

You're a loyal friend,
From what I've seen.
May your smiles never end,
Seeing them, my good fortune it's been.

Not a single moment with you has been dull,
Never a pause, never a lull.

With a wonderful warmth, you bring,
Joy, cheer and laughs that ring,
Throughout the classroom, in full swing!

Though we haven't been friends since long,
I hope that our friendship becomes strong!

May the winds of Time make you fly,
High and higher in the sky!

8th February 2019, 6pm or something

I had written this poem for my classmate, Rashmi's birthday (9th February). I saw friends giving her material things as gifts and had a desire to do something different. So, I decided to gift her with an expression of my thoughts and feelings about her. This poem was written spontaneously on a card pasted on a kite I had made and decorated.

Birthday Wishes!

A wish for you on your birthday:
Whatever you ask,
Receive you may.
Whatever you seek,
Find you may.
Whatever you wish,
May it be fulfilled on your birthday!
Stay hearty 'n' happy,
Always 'n' every day!

06th February 2019; 12:17 pm

I was reading someone else's wishes for a friend which inspired me to write this.

Happy Birthday, Ma!

Today's an auspicious day,
Ask me why, many may.
On this day, many a year back way,
A wee babe swaddled in a pink blanket lay,
Oblivious to how many demons she will have to slay,
One of many, the mother-in-law cliché.
She brought me into this world on a morn grey,
So allow me to convey,
My wishes to a person whom I obey,
Hold her above everyone else, where she will stay,
And love which won't ever go away,
To the Iron Maiden of my world today,
A very Happy Birthday!

9th January 2018, 14:40

I had written this poem for my mother's BiRtHdAy. Thanks.

Happy Birthday, Brigadier!

With a background Army green
And the stoutest dedication ever seen,
On cycling you are keen.
To maintain it, vitamins and protein,
Are your main cuisine.

A music lover, karaoke a routine.
You're always a star at the party scene.

We wish you a very Happy Birthday,
May each one be a glorious day!

13th September 2018, 12:56.

I wrote this poem on account of my father's colleague's birthday. He is a retired Army Brigadier, a fitness freak and last, but not the least, a music lover. Multi-faceted, I know, right?

Happy Birthday, Bro!

Wishing you a very happy birthday;
May each one be a glorious day.
From today, you pave the way,
To success, where your destiny lay.

Unaware, to where your destiny lies,
You never know, 'cause time flies.
Where you might end up, it's a surprise!
With age comes a nature wise,
Each day brings lows and highs.

You're one of the best guys;
May you flourish, may you rise,
Above and beyond the highest skies!

You're at the starting line for a rat race,
With new challenges to face;
Going to many an unfamiliar place;
I hope in everything you do, you ace!
Ready? Get, Set, Go!

10th September 2018, 13:57.

I wrote this poem for my elder brother's 17th Birthday.

Long Time, No Talk

Hey!
Long time, no talk.
Looks like we went on a long walk,
On the paths of our lives.
The moment of talk arrives,
Let's see if this opening survives.
If it does, we'll celebrate with high fives!
A busy schedule deprives,
Me of your company.
In my mind, it's a litany,
To find out how you are incessantly.

14th September 2018, 22:46.

Wrote this in response to a 'Hi' sent by a friend whom I haven't talked to since the beginning of this year. She's a poet too. Thanks.

Happy Teachers' Day

I wish you a Happy Teachers Day,
For our decisions, you pave the way.
You never let us go astray,
As always, steadfast you stay.
In just a few minutes, you convey,
Concepts, so life-changing that betray,
Your knowledge, wisdom and sway.
Hence, I would like to say,
Happy Teacher's Day!

4th September 2018, 22:58.

I dedicate my poem to all the teachers in our lives. They play a very crucial role: they shape our perspectives, influence our decisions and in a nutshell, decide who we are today, what kind of human being we are. With that said, I wish all, an incredibly Happy Teachers Day!

Friends

A friend like you, to me, is dear
Whom I can talk to without fear,
Of judgement, scorn or sneer.
Such friends are found so rare,
People close to you, for whom you deeply care,
That you can't help, but want your share,
Of the support, of which they have often made you
aware.
Thanks for being my friend,
I hope we will be till the end!
Happy Friendship Day!

5th August 2018, 09:16.

Written on account of Friendship Day! I woke up this morning, with this poem floating in my dreams, brought to the forefront of my mind by the realisation that today's Friendship Day. Share this poem written by me with your friends to make them feel cherished. Thanks.

Farewell to a Friend

(Dear Muskaan)
It's been great knowing you,
Though our interactions have been few.
Every time I meet you,
I learn something new,
About your love for books, thoughts;
For Shawn Mendes, you've the hots.

I agree, J K Rowling's the best,
To that fact, Harry Potter can attest.
You belong in Ravenclaw,
A wittier person, I never saw.

The time to part is upon us,
And I won't again hear you cuss,
Laugh when over grammar, you create a fuss
With friends, in the school bus.

Hope you succeed in everything you do,
Cause I'll miss you.

7th February 2020, 14:12

I had written this poem on very short notice while coming home on the bus with my friend who's about to appear for 10th grade Board exams soon and had brought a white shirt for people to sign on the last day of school. I really wanted to write something that would express my feelings towards her in a poetic way, so I hastily wrote this in about 15 minutes. Unfortunately, her stop came, and I was unable to transfer this from my notepad to her shirt. Guess I'll just send it to her through WhatsApp. Thanks.

Happy New Year!

It's time for a new year,
One which we welcome with people we hold dear.
With absolutely no fear,
We can wipe the slate completely clear,
And away from repeating mistakes past, steer.
Now, with midnight approaching near,
It's time to party with many a peer.
May this New Year bring you lots of cheer,
Along with joy so sheer!
Happy New Year!

31st December 2017, 13: 23

I wrote this poem at the urging of my mother: she wanted a unique New Year greeting.

Section IV
Chamomile (Lifestyle)

A symbol of relaxation and rest today,
Chamomile symbolised 'energy in adversity'
in the 19th century.

Fight or Flight?!

Brain says- Fight or Flight!
See the situation as a problem or plight,
And so you choose flight.
But, thinking of it as a challenge is right,
'Cause then you decide to fight!
And emerge victorious like a knight,
With a heart light, and a future bright!

9th February 2019, 10:25.

I was talking with my mother when I came up with this poem (as usual!) about the way we approach a certain situation in order to find a solution to it.

The Beauty of Simplicity

Life is a tapestry.
Each person's life is a thread.
Knots are complications created by individuals.
Each person's thread weaves itself into the tapestry,
forming a design based on his/her choices, leaving their
mark on the world.
The path, the journey or the experience depends on how
you live your life and what you do with it.
The more complicated you make your life, the more
number of knots your thread will have, making its
journey of weaving stressful/bumpy with constant
tugging and stretching, due to which your design will be
rough/disjointed and unpleasant.
Whereas, the more simple and straight you keep your
life, the more even your thread will be too, making its
journey of weaving smooth and relaxed, due to which
your design will be flowing and pleasant.
Hence,
Be simple to have a smooth-sailing,
Or complex, to be constantly complaining (and wailing).

So, it's up to you!
What kind of thread do *you* want *your* life to be -
Simple or Knotty?

5th February 2019, 13:45

Just one of my analogies and examples that I use to understand and explain things. (I know that it isn't a poem, but more of an account)

Strike a Balance

Wealth comes with Wisdom 'n' Warmth.
Keep your heart kind and good,
For, it matters what's under the hood,
Of the car, your personality 'n' behaviour.

Be magnanimous, but not too much,
For, it may often leave you in the lurch.
Be wise enough to pick your battles,
To win the war, as said by he who not tattles.

Everything's good in amounts moderate,
Hunger for power is one you can never sate,
And equality amongst all always comes late.
Strike a balance, is all that I state.

27th January 2019, 00:34.

I had saved the first line of this poem in a notepad app when it came to me 6 days back and sought to develop it further. Talking about striking a balance between everything in life is my mother's favourite topic and is also what Gautam Buddha taught.

Best Rule of Life's Game

When you're down 'n' low,
Don't look how far you've to go.
Don't lose hope,
Look how far you've come!
Who 'n' how wise a person you've become.

14th January 2019, 14:23.

I got the first 2 lines in my head while talking to my sage mother about improvement and the tough situations that she has faced in life, coming out strong and sage. The first line is from the movie The Pacifier's Peter Panda song.

When you're down in the dumps, look at those behind you, the more unfortunate, in order to boost yourself. When you feel like you're on cloud nine, look in front of you in order to aim higher. Thanks.

Spend Time and Money Wisely

Spend Time and Money wisely,
Leaving no room for regrets.
Manage time to complete jobs precisely,
And money to avoid traps and debts.

If 100 units are what you earn,
Spend 40, save 60.
This lesson is for us to learn,
To succeed in life, be thrifty.

Your time is now,
It's free and flowing
Don't let desires allow
You to drift away from knowing
Your purpose, your here and now.

Be careful with Money and Time
'Cause you reap what you sow,
The danger is at the cost of your own dime.
It can go both-high and low.

27th December 2018, 23:21.

My mother was detailing her plan on how my parents had attained financial stability after marriage when the first line of this popped into my head.

Live, Love and Laugh for that's Life

If you want others to believe in you,
You have to first believe in yourself.

If you want others to be good to you,
You've to first be good to them.

If you want others to love you,
You've to first love yourself.

If you want others to follow you,
You've to first follow your inner self.

Think of life as an experience,
Not a challenge, not a time tense.

You earn money to live,
Don't live to earn money.
So live, love and laugh,
Don't cut your joy in half.

7th December 2018, 20:12.

My mother's a very philosophical person, and I'm heavily influenced by her. She was giving me a lesson in life about how you should lead a happy life when this poem popped into my head, straining to be written down.

The Art of Joyful Living

Look for your good qualities,
There're people to look for the flaws.

If you have to step,
Step ahead,
There're people to pull you back.

If you have to dream,
Dream big,
There're people to show you your limits.

Ignite a passion that rages like a fire,
There're people to burn with envy.

If you have to make something,
Make memories.
There're people to waste time.

If you have to love,
Love yourself.
There're people to start wars.

If you have to live,
Live like a child.
There're people to make you grow up.

If you have to believe,
Believe in yourself.
There're people to doubt you.

Keep improving yourself,
There're people to show you a mirror.

Make your identity unique,
There're people to follow a crowd.

Just do something great,
Show the whole world!
There're people to applaud...

Translated on 3rd December 2018; 19:27.

I had come across an amazing and meaningful Hindi poem some time back on a social media site, a poem whose poet was not mentioned. I have translated it into English for a wider audience to enjoy the life lessons it imparts.

Responsibility and Resilience

I ask not for a lighter burden,
But for broader shoulders.
What would be said by wise men,
Of wisdom they're holders.
Helping us in the long run,
These words can move aside boulders.
Responsibility should be in everyone.
Resilience is a fire burning bright, it never smoulders.

31st July 2018, 16:26.

I know that this one doesn't seem logical; it just came out of nowhere. I was studying one minute, and the next, I'm typing this out. Hope it makes sense to you.

Call on Humanity

Looking upon an adorable puppy,
The little girl gave a sweet smile,
As refreshing as the river Nile,
Seeing it made me happy;
Though some may find me sappy,
Of joy, these are mere moments,
When these end, begin laments,
By critics, by cynics,
Of the vicious world, we live in,
Full of savages, murder and sin.

Take a look at the world around you,
It all depends on your point of view
Look for the dangers, and you'll see
Crime, death and misery
But try to look for the light,
Compassion and love make (for) a damn good sight

Here on Earth, there exists all,
The good, the bad and the ugly,

There's summer, there's fall;
It's time to take a call,
Take a chance and look for humanity.

10th February 2020, 14:29

I was preparing for my English final exam of 11th grade when I wrote this poem: While reading one of my answers for the poem "A Photograph" by Shirley Toulson, I came across the phrase 'Sweet smile' which elicited a chain of thoughts that resulted in the above poem's creation. In today's hustle-bustle, we only have time to see the dark underbelly of the world we live in: newspapers show the crime rate going up and instances of betrayal and thievery. While these try their best to erode our belief in humanity, we must remember that good things exist too. All that needs to change is our viewpoint: Look for the silver lining in every cloud yet be cautious of the shadow they bring with them. Thank you.

Existing, but Living?

We are automatons living in a world gone dead...
Running at the green, stopping at the red;
Working towards, and chasing daring dreams,
Their stress tearing our bodies apart at the seams.
Yet onward we go,
Never pausing at a yellow,
Blinded by burgeoning ambitions.

Today, money and power crack their whips,
To decide who ascends, who slips,
Down this slippery slope called success,
Which is never a permanent address.

Most humanity is no longer humane,
'Cause it's competition that talks;
Survival of the fittest as witnessed by the clocks,
With no regard to those crushed and slain.

In this world, we may be existing,
Oh, so charitably money we're giving,
But we are just pretending;

This double-faced life we are leading,
Tell me, are we really living?

In our greed for speed,
A luxurious lifestyle,
We've lost sight of our actual need,
Love and life that make us smile.

For it's not the money you amass that counts,
When the bill comes due,
But the lives you brighten that amounts,
To a life well lived with happiness, old and new.

30th January 2020, 22:54.

I didn't mean to write this poem when I sat down to write originally (I wanted to write a short couplet on my personality for a social media site's profile but couldn't find a flow of thoughts). After reading my own creation, I found it quite relevant in today's era of busyness and the fast-paced lives that we seem to live. Nowadays, winning and success matter more than someone's emotions and these have turned us into machines that work and work with no proper downtime. So I suggest you spend some happy time with your family once in a while cause these are the moments that actually count (To die alone in a wealthy hospital versus dying with your loved ones there beside you, i.e. money provides a cold comfort in times of need, it's family that really helps) Thanks.

Reach Out to Play

You have to step onto the field,
If you want to play the game.
Step out of your comfort zone
And see the results you'll yield
It'll be yours: Fortune n Fame
To call these your own,
Explore something new once in a while
Something that helps you grow
So you'll have some laurels to show
At the end of the line.
For it's my wish, dear friend mine,
To see you go out in style.

Well, what do you say?
Will you reach out to play?

24th January 2020, 17:20

I got the first 2 lines in my head when I wanted to tell a junior schoolmate that he could not become a General in the

Indian Army if he wasn't willing to take the risk of having to lay down his life in the line of duty. (My father served in the Army for 22 years). You can't grow in a field unless you reach for something new to keep you going. You need to be willing to accept the risks that come with every field in order to play and excel in it. Thanks.

Forgive, but Never Forget

If others wrong you,
Forgive them,
But never forget
The lessons you learnt
When their deeds burnt
Your belief in them.

If you forgive and forget,
Tis an act of foolishness,
For every time you face their misdeeds,
You'll be surprised, and your heart bleeds.

So don't forget, but do forgive,
For these are people with whom you have to live.
It's not that they're worth your pardon and release,
But that you deserve proper peace.

10th January 2020, 11:33.

I wrote this poem while discussing with my mother the wrong deeds of people who hurt us and why we should forgive them for our peace of mind but never forget the lessons that we learn from their harmful actions. Thanks.

Learn to Learn

You need to be humble to learn something,
If it's success and stature you want to earn;
Open up yourself to a person,
If you wish to receive their teaching
For, arrogance and ego are the barriers,
To true learning and lessons;
They restrict the knowledge-carriers,
From sharing their enlightened minds
The student must bow and bend,
If ignorance and darkness were to end.

In the world of egos and conflicts,
If all of us learn how to learn;
Life will blossom, and egos won't hurt.

29th April 2020, 14:11

A thought had occurred to me when I was unable to fully grasp an English lesson (The Enemy by Pearl S. Buck) after reading it. I wondered why this was so and realised that I wouldn't be able to completely LEARN its deeper meaning unless and until I have let go of my arrogant thought that I'm ahead in comprehension with regard to my class. This inner conversation made me think:

You need to be humble to learn,

For it's knowledge you'll earn.

These two lines were inspired by something I had read or heard somewhere 2-3 years ago. Thanks.

Section V
Magnolia (Nature)

This flower symbolises love for nature along with dignity (purple), perseverance, affection (pink), spirituality (white) and friendship (yellow).

A Magnificent Morning

Together as one,
The eagles fly towards the sun,
In the morning mist, to feast.
Dawn is to go towards the east,
Dusk is to return back west;
Home, back to their nest.

Eagles are the best,
Skilled predators, fierce mothers.
Like these majestic birds, there're no others.

8th December 2018, 10:24.

I was playing badminton with my mother in the early morning today. We were just finishing up when we saw a fleet of eagles swoop as one, painting a broad stroke across the sky. My mother told me about their travel to the east in the mornings and to the west in the evenings, which is what prompted me to write this poem. I hope you enjoy it.

Sensory Overload!

Wafting past me is the smell of achaar,
Helpless in the backseat, hoon main laachaar.
Surrounded by lush shrubs n green,
My mood serene,
Thinking this is what you mean,
By sensory overload.

Assailed by the wind blowing past,
My window, drying my hair at last.

The rustle 'n' hustle of the breeze,
Lulling me to sleep,
With shoulders relaxed, at ease.

Away from the stressful city,
I thought, gained clarity,
And ran away with alacrity!

Can't stay here forever,
Oh! What a pity!

Hills n valleys all around,
Where peace 'n' quiet abound,
With nature's melody, the only sound.

8th September 2018, 12:57.

I went on a road trip with my family recently and had washed my hair before leaving in the wee hours of the morning. Travelling on an Expressway, I saw, heard, smelled and felt my surroundings. It inspired me to write this poem.

Nature's Bounty

Bright flowers blooming in the sunshine,
While vines in tangles with each other twine.
In a field full of trees,
Stand empty husks that no longer buzz with bees.

The turbulent sky dotted with nary a wispy cloud,
Witness to the wind that whistles so loud.
There's a bite to the chilly morning air,
Blowing upon a maiden equally fair.

So fertile is the wet mud,
For our Earth, it is precious blood.
Even better is the soil,
In which for hours do the farmers toil.

The plants growing a lovely green,
To them, storms can be terribly mean.
Dotted with clouds, streaked with dying sun rays,
is the sky,
Heaven 'n' Earth does it tie.

Of Nature's bounty,
We have always been the taker,
Greed for more, from every town to county.
Discontent with treasure bestowed upon us
by our Maker.

All the world's a stage,
Is Mother Nature a mage?
Lending our lives, a constant maze,
Yes! It never ceases to amaze.

Mother Nature's wealth,
Is what we carelessly squander,
At night by stealth,
While to unknown places we wander.

Nature is now tainted with concrete,
Which it doesn't consider a treat.
So, save nature's pure beauty,
And fulfil your duty!

4th July 2017

Another of my school activities: Write a poem based on nature after seeing the scenic (not) view available to students, teachers and staff.

Section VI
Purple Crocus (Studies)

The first sign of spring, the purple crocus symbolises youthful happiness and knowledge.

Exams Enter, Exams Exit

Free from exams!
A temporary reprieve,
Is what we receive,
With open arms!

Exams enter, exams exit;
Don't lose hope.
There's always the next one!
Life is an endless exam,
You may pass in some,
But can fail too.
It's this contrast that keeps us going,
For constant success leads to arrogance,
And frequent failure to hopelessness.
A success enables us to celebrate,
A failure teaches us to improve.

And so my friend,
Let's celebrate the end,
Of this round, this fleet/wave;
And gear up for the next one!

21st December 2018, 23:52.

I wrote this poem right now, with today being my last preliminary exam: I'm **FREE!!!** *This sentiment is what I wanted to express in this poem. Also, the fact that this exam isn't everything and that we shouldn't think that all our exams are over for exams are never-ending, they just change their forms just like energy. Thanks.*

Quaking Quills

Tick. Tock. Tick. Tock.
The deadline approaches near.
The ever-moving hands of the clock.
To the exam, I look with fear.

5th December 2018, 11:47

I wrote this short poem during a workshop on Study Skills and Exam Anxiety. The counsellor had asked us to calculate the number of days left for our BOARD exams (92 days) as according to her, it will help us prepare better, but I don't share her opinion. I feel that if you keep a countdown, it'll take a toll on you, increasing the pressure when the months left turn into weeks and finally, days. Time flies when you're happy, and it flies when you're apprehensive and scared.

You're Not Cool Anymore

You're not cool anymore
You're not cool anymore
You're not cool anymore
Like you used to be

I don't like you anymore
What was all of it for
Oh. You're not cool anymore
Like you used to be.

I just heard you have lost your marbles now
You have been losing for a while
Wish I would've known a bit before
Cause even after all this time I still wonder,
What has happened to you
That every day for me is a chore...

Don't wanna know,
Kind of work was done in class,
If the homework is given in amounts mass
The way it is now

I had relaxed,
Should've known your pace was a game,
Now I can't get you out of my brain
Oh, it's such a shame...

That You're not cool anymore
You're not cool anymore
You're not cool anymore
Like you used to be

I don't like you anymore
What was all of it for
Oh. You're not cool anymore
Like you used to be.

I just hope you've realized your mistake,
Which was a great error in judgement
There is a good reason that you're wrong
Every now and then I think you might want me to help
you change your ways
But I'm just too afraid that I'll be wrong

Don't wanna know
If you have a scheme that will suffice,
If it will bring you back from this precipice
To how you were before

I had relaxed
Should've known your pace was a game
Now I can't get you out of my brain
Oh it's such a shame

That You're not cool anymore
You're not cool anymore
You're not cool anymore
Like you used to be.

15th May 2018, 23:05.

This is written with respect to my school, which, unfortunately, is not so cool anymore. This is based on the song, "We Don't Talk Anymore" by Charlie Puth and Selena Gomez. I have always been a person who enjoys going to school, a reason why I'm really frustrated that my school has changed its wonderful ways to something harmful to student's mental and physical health.

Worrying About What Lies Ahead

My eyes are red,
With maths, I'm up fed.
With feet like lead,
I just want to go to bed.

I'm hanging on by a thread,
To my focus in keeping my head.

The greatest test is coming ahead.
All my textbooks have been read,
But it's with dread,
That today I go to bed.
Wondering if I will proceed ahead,
In life, in the path that I've led.

20th March 2018, 21:37 pm.

I wrote this poem in a troubled state of mind as you can probably guess from the poem. I had failed my 9th grade final maths exam because of health issues and had been preparing rigorously for the retest that was to be held on 21st March 2018. This poem was written the night before the retest that would decide whether I would continue on to the 10th grade or be held back in the 9th grade with students I thought of as my juniors. Thanks.

Thoughts on the Last Exam

The last exam is what this is all about,
Of exams, the elephant's out;
What's left behind, is its tail,
To push out which we continue to flail,
Studying morning, evening yet to no avail.

As I lie down this night,
I hope my frantic efforts will prevail,
Towards the next level, let my boat sail;
A new journey, a damn good sight,
To set out for with a heart light,
With friends, and a future beaming bright.

25th February 2020, 21:16

I was about to appear for the last exam of 11th grade the next day and couldn't wait to get it over with, with 7 days of holiday heaven just within my reach. The first 4 lines are based on a Hindi proverb (हाथी निकल गया लेकिन उसकी पूँछ रह गई) meaning the event is almost over, only its end is yet to come, an end that is very hard to go through because of frustration and anticipation. Thanks.

School: A Nocturnal Poem

A place called the school,
Where discipline & learning rule.
It's a place where we come to learn,
A good education here we earn.

Getting a good education can be fun,
In a few years, it is done.
A place first entered as a child,
Whose imagination runs wild.

Where children nurture their personality
And build their potential for versatility.
Like how a mother cares for her child every day,
A teacher cares for her student the same way.

Some schools are interested in mathematics,
While some are dedicated to athletics.
There are numerous schools,
But common are the teaching tools.

There are thousands of schools spread worldwide,
That bring about education in waves of tide.
These days of school can be progressive,
To prepare us for life may get aggressive.

This is a chance not everybody gets,
But that is something one often forgets.
Here we may make a lifelong friend,
One whose back we have till the end.

School is an important institution,
Where we develop a sense of intuition.

These years cannot be redone,
They are yours to cherish.
Treasured should be each one,
So, don't let a single day perish...

July 2017

You can probably guess from the title that the poem has something to do with the night. The inspiration for this poem struck me at midnight one day 7 months ago, so I recorded it on my phone and wrote it down the next morning. Not many realise the importance of schools and receiving an education as it was easily given to them. This opportunity to gain education and skills in order to earn a livelihood is precious for those facing poverty. Hence, we should be grateful to have been given such a boon.

Section VII
Rosemary (Food)

A symbol of remembrance, the leaves of this herb are used to flavour various foods like stuffing and roast meats.

Mission Hunger to Sate

Let's pick up a plate
We're getting late
And It's time we ate
Enough of the wait
The buffet's been laid
Bhuka he mera pet (Translation: My stomach is hungry)
Look at the delicious dishes made
Bread, Butter, marmalade
Preserves of every shade
Available right at your fingertips
So lick your lips,
And feast on this buffet!

Platters of bountiful fruits,
Plenty of opportunities for foodies to loot.
So it's with glee that we hoot,
And strain the buttons of our monkey suits.

Mission Hunger to Sate,
Is operational from this date!

8th September 2018, 08:36.

I wrote this poem after partaking of a delectable buffet in Mumbai. I'm a foodie and usually write poems in English, but some like this one and Sensory Overload are a mix of English and Hinglish (Hindi and English). Hope you enjoy this verbal feast!

Eat Right, Feel Light

If your waistband is tight,
Never go on a diet,
For, you just have to eat right!

At breakfast, feast like a king;
At lunch, a medium meal is the right thing;
At dinner, eat a supper light;
All-day, keep yourself hydrated and light.

In your chest, let hope alight,
That one day soon, you'll feel light as a kite!

So, my dear friend,
Insecurity will end,
If you eat right,
To feel light!

July 2018, 10:55

I wrote this poem while my school principal lectured my class on stress management and healthy habits. Hope you follow her dictates, or else, there'll be a hefty price to pay!

My Birthday Cake

It's my birthday tonight,
With a soft golden light,
Bathing my cake in colours virginal white.
To my utter delight,
The cake, vanilla, a flavour light,
Melts in my mouth, soft as butter might.
A strawberry dollop sits not as a blight
But at the top centre like a red cherry tight
The burning candle has to fight,
To keep burning, it's wick bright

26th May 2018, 20:17

I wrote this short poem after coming face to face with my birthday cake for the first time. I'm a foodie, something you can probably glean from the fact that I wrote an ode to my cake. But what a delectable cake it was!

Philosophy for Foodies

Life is like a buffet table,
Many experiences are available
It's up to you what you wish to pick,
Pick one you wish to evermore stick
To your personality, your plate
For it determines your fate.

23rd March 2018, 14:40

Just an analogy for life that came to mind while talking to my sage mother.

Section VIII
Violet (Family)

*This flower symbolises loyalty,
devotion and faithfulness.*

My Dear Brother

My dear brother
Your name means the Sun,
Being around you is quite fun,
Know that you are a cherished one.

Your disposition is sunny,
Jokes you crack are funny.
Engineering is your passion!
You don't care a whit about fashion.

You're very caring,
But can, in a second turn daring.
You've a personality so charming,
Towards which people come swarming.

In academics, so studious,
With promises, so fastidious.
My dear bright sun,
You're a cherished one.

28th August 2016, 11:28a.m.

This poem is based on my brother. I had written this for his 10th grade farewell party on the urging of my History teacher Kavya Ma'am. This was the poem that cleared the block/garbage that could have been clogging my creative pipes as after writing this, I wrote 2 more on the same day. My creative juices now flow at completely unexpected times.

My Loving Mum

You work so hard my loving mum,
Dishes made by you are yum.
Your teachings are knowledgeable,
You save whatever is forageable.

You are very caring,
But can, in a second turn daring.
With an iron will,
Fear in the hearts of bullies you instil,
You protect us from a disguised devil.

You gave me life,
More than enough to suffice,
And are a dutiful wife,
With former slaps as sharp as a knife.

You are someone to cherish,
May the people who harm you perish!
Your disposition is sunny,
Jokes you crack are funny!

You're hard outside,
And soft inside,
But you never say anything snide.

Watching your temper flare,
To make a noise, I wouldn't dare!
With me having a fever,
You're God's firm believer.

You're my beautiful factory,
And I'm your victory,
Having completed a duty which is history,
Who decided that is a mystery!

With you being so loving,
Every moment with you is moving

28th August 2016, 12:04.

I dedicate this poem to my mother. I wrote this poem in school during History period under my desk.

Dearest Dad

Dearest dad,
Saving me from people with intentions bad,
Who make me sad.

You are a linguist,
Gave discipline a new twist.
Fitness is your passion,
While being in fashion.

In many ways I resemble you,
Well, that is not new,
With differences being so few,
You'd like The Taming of the Shrew.

You work hard and flourish,
While those who condemn you perish.
Run Daddy! Run! We chant,
For running is your penchant.

You don't in a place settle,
And sometimes people you nettle,
For everybody does a little!

You care a lot dearest dad,
Saving me from people with intentions bad,
Who make me sad,
Thanks for being there, Dad!

28th August 2016, 12:32 pm.

I dedicate this poem to my father. I had written it in my school bus while returning home.

The Warning of a Wise Woman

I may look sweet,
But don't try to disturb my life neat,
For, you may find to your dismay complete,
That I can pull the rug from under your feet.

Mine is an existence bittersweet,
Win my loyalty 'n' you are in for a treat,
For, a more kind person you can't ever meet.
But beware, make me a fool, or cheat,
And I'll kick you to the street!
In size, I may be petite,
But looks can be deceptive,
As I make of fools mincemeat.

Consider this as a warning,
Don't mess with me, an omen,
Heed it, heed this forewarning,
The Warning of a Wise Woman.

5th March 2018, 11:29 am.

I dedicate this poem to the Wise Woman in my life, my lovely mother. She is the one who inspired me to write this poem from her perspective.

My Brave Brother

I see him itch to play,
A fight he fights every day.
I hope that one day he may,
With his arm steady, play.

These fears are his dragons to slay,
Bloody on the pavement, to splay.

The thought he could never again (play) does weigh,
Heavy on our hearts with dismay.

Now his arm will be okay,
He's making headway,
Towards recovery on Christmas day.

With a rod in his arm,
And burdens on his shoulders,
My brother's passing every exam,
Making himself stronger and bolder.

24th December 2018, 19:44.

I typed this poem while taking a walk in my society with my brother. He loves to play tennis but cannot do so presently due to an accident that broke both of the bones (radius 'n' ulna) in his right arm. Hence, he has a rod and a plate inserted into his arm, an operation that took place 6 months back. He goes to meet his tennis instructor whenever we walk past the court, and it is this yearning of his that made me write this poem.

Silencing Silence

With problems, when acceptance doesn't tag along,
There's right, and there's wrong.
Doubt's high, and distance, a mile long.
Both yearn to rejoice in serenity's song,
Yet their silence is far too strong.

9th January 2020, 11:04.

I wrote this in school after reading Elizabeth Jenning's Father to Son poem. Acceptance is hard to come by, while lack of communication abounds these days.... estranged families have increased their numbers, aided by the concept of nuclear families. The title is inspired by the last line of Shirley Toulson's A Photograph ("Its silence silences").

Section IX
Lotus (Mother Tongue)

*The national flower of India, the Lotus
is regarded in eastern religions, as a symbol
of purity, enlightenment, self-regeneration
and rebirth.*

एक माँ की दास्तान

हाँ मेरी जान
मैं हूँ बड़ी पहलवान
काम से नहीं होती मैं परेशान
अब काम करना ही है हमारी शान
उसे अच्छे से करने में ही है मेरी आन
अपने हर काम पे न्योछावर है मेरी दिलो-जान
क्योंकि ऐसे नागरिकों से ही बनेगा खुशहाल हिन्दुस्तान
मेरी जरूरतें हैं मोहब्बत और मान
अपनों को देती हूँ अपने दिल में स्थान।
मेरा परिवार ही है मेरा जहान
मेरा जहान, मेरी पहचान।

English Translation:

A Mother's Tale

Yes, my dear,
I'm strong, don't fear
Work doesn't bother me
For it is in work that lies my pride

Doing it right is my successful stride.
Into every chore, I pour my complete soul
For only such citizens will make India a flourishing whole.
All I need is love and respect,
Loved ones are close to my heart.
My family is my whole world
My world, my identity.

3rd January 2020, 13:37

Written from my mother's perspective by me, about her daily hard work that's put into our family life. I've added a rough translation of the original poem so that it can be read by a wider audience as well. Thanks.

विश्वास

कोई तुम पर इतना विश्वास करे,
इसका तुम्हें एहसास रहे,
कि तुम्हारी ज़िम्मेदारी तुम से कहे,
यह विश्वास, बना रहे।

4 June 2019, 10:04

Translated in English:

Belief

When someone has so much faith in you,
It's prudent that you realize its importance,
That your responsibility urges you,
May this belief remain ever-long.

25th January 2020, 10:00

I had been reading the newspaper when this poem struck me suddenly. To hold one's faith is a precious gift that many may take for granted but one that needs to be upheld. Thanks.

नम नयन

हो आँखो में नमी,
बस पलकों पर है,
इसके आने की कमी,
कि इन्हें पोंछदू मैं।

9th February 2020, 21:03

English translation:

Moist Eyes

There's wetness in your eyes,
A grievance you can't say,
That your eyelids need only express,
For me to wipe it away.

9th February 2020, 22:34

I wrote this after watching Dharmendra (a veteran Bollywood actor) get teary-eyed at one of his famous songs being sung by a pair of participants in a singing show (called Indian Idol) where he was present as a guest. I guess I meant to convey that you need to open up to a close one about your wounds and grievances to allow them to heal, be comforted and be addressed properly. Thank you.

धन्यवाद

आपकी शुभ कामनाओं के लिए धान्यवाद,
यह हमेशा रहेंगी मेरे साथ,
जीवन में थामेंगी मेरा हाथ,
कि खुशनुमा होगा मेरा सफर।

9th January 2020, 17:15.

I wrote this poem in response to the birthday wishes showered upon my mother, as a response from her side to express her heartfelt gratitude to have received such blessings. Thanks

जिंदगी की एक सीख

आसान है दूसरों पर हँसना,
मुश्किल है, तो कुछ करके दिखाना।

3rd January 2018, 16:34

Translated in English:

A Life Lesson

It's easy to laugh at others,

What's difficult is to do something worthwhile.

I got this line in my mind when I saw a 6th grader laughing at his classmate for mispronouncing a word in his storytelling in the school bus while coming back home. Unfortunately, I couldn't say this to him as his stop had come immediately after this incident. I feel that this is something we should all remember when we are laughed at or when we are the ones who do the mocking, a position I hope at least I'm never in.

विचारों की कठपुतली

इन्सान होता है विचारों की कठपुतली,
यह बिगड़े, तो जीवन की दिशा बदली
यह सुधारें, तो जीवन की दशा सुधार गई।

अब इन्सान करता ही क्या है,
अपने हाथों सहित काम?
और इन हाथों को कौन चलाता है,
है तो एक खयाल ही ना?

English Translation:

A Puppet of Thoughts

A person is a mere puppet of thoughts,
When these degrade, life takes a dark turn;
When these uplift, life improves and lightens.

What does a person actually do,
Work with their hands, right?

And who controls these hands,
It's a thought after all, isn't it?

14th April 2020, 13:48.

I wrote this poem while cleaning methi (fenugreek) for lunch and discussing with my mother about the significant role thoughts play in one's life and how the change in one's thoughts can change their very life. I was being assailed by strange and negative thoughts even about positive and loving situations which worried me a lot and which had to be rejected immediately to not take root. One example of such a negative change and its adverse effects can be seen in Ramayan, i.e. Kekayi's case. She was a loving mother whose mind had been corrupted by her handmaid Meneka, towards Kaushalya's son Ram. Thanks.

Gratitude

To my dear reader,

Congratulations! You have finished my book of poetry!

I'm so glad that you decided to read my book and stuck with it till the end. I hope that you enjoyed it and that it may have offered something new to you.

Do tell your friends about my book if you think that they will be interested in reading it since word-of-mouth is an essential way for readers to discover and read the work of new authors like me.

Send me a selfie of yourself with a copy of my book at my email address, i.e. aanchalg265@gmail.com. I would love to create a collage comprising of my readers, so as to always remember each of you.

I would love to hear your views about my poems, so please feel free to share your views with me, either through a book review at the respective site store or through my email address.

(P.S. I absolutely *love* collecting photographs and reminiscing about the moments captured within them; I take very frequent trips down a deeply-trodden memory lane, often with my like-minded family.)

With warm regards,
Aanchal Gupta